Captain's Log

Andrew Solway

www.raintreepublishers.co.uk

Visit our website to find out more information about **Raintree** books.

To order:

☎ Phone 44 (0) 1865 888112

🖹 Send a fax to 44 (0) 1865 314091

💻 Visit the Raintree bookshop at **www.raintreepublishers.co.uk** to browse our catalogue and order online.

First published in Great Britain by Raintree, Halley Court, Jordan Hill, Oxford OX2 8EJ, part of Harcourt Education.

Raintree is a registered trademark of Harcourt Education Ltd.

Editorial: Louise Galpine, Harriet Milles, and Rachel Howells
Design: Richard Parker and Tinstar Design www.tinstar.co.uk
Illustrations: International Mapping
Picture Research: Hannah Taylor
Production: Alison Parsons
Originated by Modern Age
Printed and bound in China by Leo Paper Group

13-digit ISBN 978 1 4062 0841 2 (hardback)
12 11 10 09 08
10 9 8 7 6 5 4 3 2 1

13-digit ISBN 978 1 4062 0848 1 (paperback)
12 11 10 09 08
10 9 8 7 6 5 4 3 2 1

British Library Cataloguing in Publication Data
Solway, Andrew
    Captain's log. - (Fusion history)
    1. Explorers - England - History - 16th century
Juvenile literature 2. Discoveries in geography
English - History - 16th century - Juvenile literature
I. Title
910.9'1
A full catalogue record for this book is available from the British Library

Acknowledgements
The publishers would like to thank the following for permission to reproduce photographs: Alamy Images (Nigel Reed) p. **11**; Bridgeman Art Library pp. **5** (The Crown Estate), **6**, **15**, **19**, **23** (Private Collection); Corbis pp. **7** (Adam Woolfitt), **8** (National Gallery Collection) **12** (Historical Picture Archive), **24** (Joel.W Rogers); Mary Evans Picture Library pp. **14**, **17**, **21**, **27**; National Maritime Museum p. **13**.

Cover photograph of the *Golden Hind* reproduced with permission of Corbis/Joel W. Rogers.

Every effort has been made to contact copyright holders of any material reproduced in this book. Any omissions will be rectified in subsequent printings if notice is given to the publishers.

The publishers would like to thank Bill Mariott and Lynne Bold for their assistance with the preparation of this book.

Disclaimer
All the Internet addresses (URLs) given in this book were valid at the time of going to press. However, due to the dynamic nature of the Internet, some addresses may have changed, or sites may have changed or ceased to exist since publication. While the author and publishers regret any inconvenience this may cause readers, no responsibility for any such changes can be accepted by either the author or the publishers.

It is recommended that adults supervise children on the Internet.

Contents

Some words are printed in bold, **like this**. You can find out what they mean on page 30. You can also look in the box at the bottom of the page where they first appear.

Top secret!

What happened to Francis Drake's **logbook**? It is a mystery that is over 400 years old.

Francis Drake was a famous ship's captain and an **explorer**. He lived during the **reign** of Queen Elizabeth I. In 1577 he sailed around the world. This amazing sea voyage lasted nearly three years.

The background story

In 1577, England and Spain were at peace. But they were not friendly. Spain was rich and powerful. The Spanish had **colonies** in South America. There was gold and silver there. The Spanish took this treasure by ship up the Pacific coast of South America (see map, right). It crossed Panama by mule. Then it sailed across the Atlantic to Spain. Spanish ships sailing the Atlantic were heavily guarded. But the ships sailing up the Pacific coast were not.

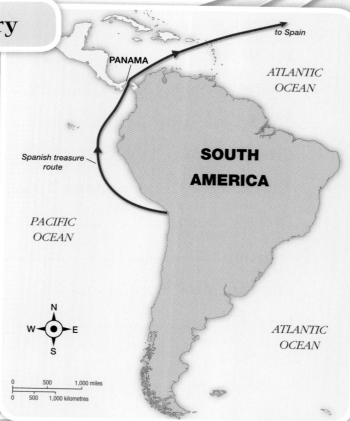

to Spain

PANAMA

ATLANTIC OCEAN

Spanish treasure route

SOUTH AMERICA

PACIFIC OCEAN

ATLANTIC OCEAN

N
W   E
S

| 0 | 500 | 1,000 miles |
| 0 | 500 | 1,000 kilometres |

4

This picture shows Drake as he probably looked at the time of his voyage.

A captain's logbook is like a diary. It tells the story of a voyage. Drake gave the logbook of his amazing voyage to Queen Elizabeth I. It has not been seen since then.

Today, we know some details of Drake's voyage. Some of his crew wrote about the voyage. Some talked to people about it. But the logbook is still missing.

This is the story of what might have been in that logbook – and why it was top secret!

Setting sail

It is November 1577. We are in Plymouth, Devon. In the harbour are five small sailing ships. Their names are the *Pelican*, the *Elizabeth*, the *Marigold*, the *Swan*, and the *Christopher*.

Sailors are loading supplies for a long voyage. They are loading beer, water, and salted meat. There are carpenters' tools, wood, and ropes. There are candles, buckets, and needles.

In this picture, Sir Francis Drake is watching his ship, the Pelican, *being loaded.*

Now all the supplies and people are on board. The ships are ready to go. The captain, Francis Drake, is on the *Pelican*. He gives the order to sail. Slowly, the little **fleet** of ships begins its long journey.

The *Mary Rose*

In July 1545, a large warship called the *Mary Rose* sank near Portsmouth. The ship's wreck was finally lifted from the seabed in 1982. Inside the wreck were some of the sailors' personal belongings. You can see some of these in the photo above. It shows coins, a whistle, dice, and a leather pouch. These can now be seen in a museum in Portsmouth.

False start

Not far from Plymouth the **fleet** meets terrible weather. They have to turn back. In December they set out once more. Two weeks later they are sailing down the coast of Africa.

Most of the crew think they are going to Egypt. Now Drake tells them the truth. They are sailing to the Pacific Ocean. They are going to attack Spanish treasure ships. Drake promises the crew riches and adventure. Some of the sailors are angry. Others like the idea of Spanish treasure!

Sailing in storms like this is very dangerous. Drake and his crew had to wait for the bad weather to finish before returning to Plymouth to repair the fleet.

pilot   on a ship, someone who decides which way a ship should

The fleet sails to the Cape Verde Islands. There they capture a Portuguese ship. They let the crew go, but they keep the ship and its **pilot**. Then they set off west across the Atlantic.

Life on board

Drake's ships were tiny, and very uncomfortable. The sailors had no beds. They slept on sails, sacks, or even coils of rope! Food could not be kept fresh. On long voyages sailors ate salted meat and hard biscuits. They drank beer when they had it. Beer keeps fresh better than water.

This map shows the first part of Drake's voyage. The Pelican *sails from Plymouth to the Cape Verde Islands.*

ATLANTIC OCEAN

ENGLAND
Plymouth Portsmouth

Drake's route

EUROPE

SPAIN

Canary Islands

Mediterranean Sea

N
W — E
S

EGYPT

0   1,000   2,000 miles
0   1,000   2,000 kilometres

Cape Verde Islands

AFRICA

Trouble on board!

Drake's **fleet** of ships sail across the Atlantic Ocean. They reach South America in April 1578. But one man is causing trouble. His name is Thomas Doughty. Before the voyage, Doughty worked for Sir Christopher Hatton. Sir Christopher gave Drake money for the voyage.

At first Drake trusted Doughty. He made him captain of the *Swan*. Later he made him captain of his own ship, the *Pelican*.

But on the *Pelican* Doughty complains about Drake. He says that Drake should not be captain of the fleet. Doughty tells the crew to leave Drake. He says they should go treasure-hunting on their own.

Finally Drake decides he has had enough. The fleet stops at Port St. Julian in Argentina. Drake puts Doughty on **trial**. He accuses him of **treason**. The **jury** is the ship's crew. They decide Doughty is guilty. He is **beheaded** on 2 July 1578.

behead to kill someone by chopping off their head
figurehead figure at the front part of a ship
jury group of people who decide whether someone is guilty or innocent in a trial
treason action that is disloyal to your country
trial special meeting to decide if someone is guilty or innocent of a crime

In 1578, Drake changes the name of his ship to the Golden Hind. He gives it a new **figurehead** of a deer (hind), like this one.

The second part of Drake's voyage takes him to the tip of South America.

SOUTH AMERICA

BOLIVIA

CHILE

Valparaiso

ARGENTINA

Drake's route

ATLANTIC OCEAN

Port St. Julian

N
W ◆ E
S

0   1,000   2,000 miles

0   1,000   2,000 kilometres

Into the Pacific

Two ships are damaged on the trip down the coast of Argentina. They are the *Christopher* and the *Swan*. Drake has to leave them behind. He reaches the tip of South America with only three ships.

Now the ships have to sail through the narrow **Strait** of Magellan. They wind their way between hundreds of rocky islands.

This old map of the Strait of Magellan shows how difficult it was for Drake's ships to sail through.

lead line weight on a thin rope that is thrown over the side of a ship to measure water depth
strait narrow strip of water between two pieces of land

A sailor uses a **lead line** to measure the water depth. He needs to know that the water is deep enough for the ships to pass through.

On 6 September 1578 the **fleet** reaches open water. They are in the Pacific Ocean! No English ships have ever been here before. But almost straight away they are hit by a storm.

The unknown Pacific

In 1578, hardly anything was known about the vast Pacific Ocean. Three Spanish ships sailed that way before Drake. None of the Spanish captains made good maps. Drake kept careful records on his voyage. He filled in some of the blank areas on the world map.

← *This sailor uses a lead line. One end of the rope has a weight on it. He will throw this end into the water. Strips of material on the rope mark out the water depth.*

Storms and losses

The storm is terrible. Strong winds blow from the north. They push the three ships southwards. The waves are like mountains of water. The storm goes on for days and days.

After about two weeks, the *Marigold* sinks with her whole crew. Soon afterwards, the *Elizabeth* and the *Golden Hind* are separated. The *Elizabeth* turns and sails back to England. Only the *Golden Hind* goes on.

The Marigold *sank in stormy seas in the Pacific. This picture shows a similar sinking.*

Native Americans   the original people of North

Meeting the locals

In many places where Drake landed, there were Native Americans. Drake always tried to be friendly. He offered them gifts. But the Araucanian Native Americans in southern Chile were at war with the Spanish. The Spanish had invaded their lands. They attacked Drake and his crew because they thought they were Spanish. In this picture (above), a Native American steals Drake's hat!

The storm lasts for 56 days. Afterwards, Drake finds himself in a wide southern ocean. The *Golden Hind* heads north. In southern Chile Drake finds a place to repair the ship. There are **Native Americans** living there. They seem friendly at first. But one day they attack a group from the ship. Two sailors are killed.

Spanish raids

It is December 1578. Drake has now reached lands where the Spanish have **settlements**. He hears from some **Native Americans** that there is a Spanish ship in the port of Valparaiso. He sails boldly into the port and boards the ship. At first the ship's crew think Drake and his men are Spaniards. They soon find out their mistake! Drake takes the crew prisoner.

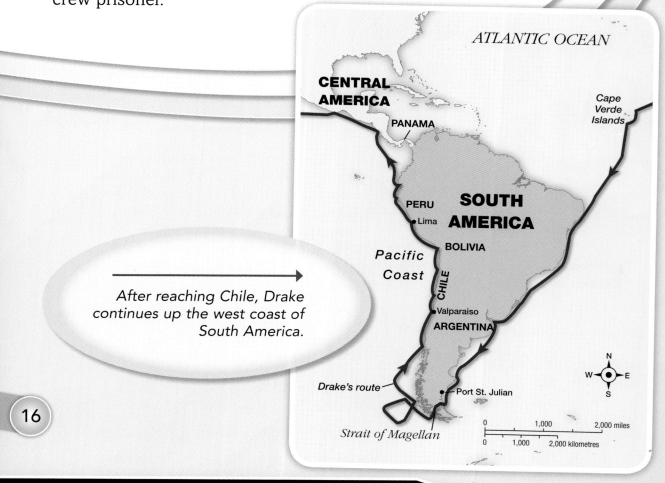

After reaching Chile, Drake continues up the west coast of South America.

ATLANTIC OCEAN

CENTRAL AMERICA

PANAMA

Cape Verde Islands

PERU
Lima

SOUTH AMERICA

BOLIVIA

Pacific Coast

CHILE

Valparaiso

ARGENTINA

Drake's route

Port St. Julian

N
W · E
S

Strait of Magellan

0   1,000   2,000 miles
0   1,000   2,000 kilometres

ransom money paid to set a prisoner free
settlement town or village

Next Drake and his crew attack the town. The few people who live there run away. Drake takes gold, silver, and other goods from the ship and the town.

After Valparaiso, Drake attacks several more ports. He captures many Spanish ships. He collects more and more treasure. Usually he lets the crew go. But sometimes he takes a rich Spaniard prisoner. He demands a **ransom** from the Spanish to set the prisoner free.

Well-treated prisoners

Some Spanish prisoners wrote about being captured by Drake. Nearly all of them said Drake treated them very well. He often invited them to eat with him in his cabin. This picture (right) shows a Spanish gentleman from the 1600s. The men Drake captured may have dressed like this.

A rich prize

On 15 February 1579, the *Golden Hind* reaches Lima in Peru. Here Drake hears some exciting news. A Spanish ship called the *Cacafuego* has recently passed through. It is carrying silver.

Drake decides to chase the *Cacafuego*. On 1 March he sees a sail on the horizon. It is the ship!

Drake sails the *Golden Hind* slowly. He pretends that he is just passing by. The crew of the *Cacafuego* are fooled. They think there is no danger. When Drake gets close to the treasure ship, he shows his guns. He tells the *Cacafuego* to surrender. But the captain of the *Cacafuego* puts up a fierce fight before he gives up.

On board the *Cacafuego* there is a vast fortune of gold, coins, and jewellery. There is also over 20 tonnes of silver!

Making space

The bottom of a Tudor sailing ship was filled with large stones called **ballast**. The ballast balanced the weight of the masts. Drake captured a lot of treasure on the *Cacafuego*. He had to empty out the ballast on the *Golden Hind* to make room for it. The ballast on Drake's ship was silver!

In this picture, Drake captures the Spanish treasure ship the Cacafuego. Drake comes alongside the ship, and then opens fire.

19

Which way home?

Now Drake's ship is full of treasure. He decides it is time to go home to England. But he cannot go back the way he came. He is sure to meet Spanish ships after his blood! Drake sails the *Golden Hind* northwards up the west coast of the Americas.

Some of Drake's maps show a sea passage right through North America. But he cannot find this northwest passage. They must go home the long way, westwards across the Pacific Ocean. But first the ship needs food, water, and repairs.

In June 1579, Drake finds a quiet bay. The **Native Americans** in the area are very friendly. They crown Drake king, and give him many gifts. Drake claims this land for Queen Elizabeth I. He calls it "Nova Albion" ("New Britain").

Nova Albion

No one knows exactly where Drake's "Nova Albion" was. Some people think it was on the Pacific coast of California in the United States. Others think it was on the coast of Oregon. This map shows where people think it might be.

In Nova Albion, Drake and his crew meet Native Americans. They get on very well with Drake. Here Drake is given a Native American crown.

21

The Spice Islands

Drake leaves Nova Albion at the end of July. It takes him two months to cross the Pacific Ocean. In October 1579, the ship reaches a small group of islands not far from New Guinea. The people are friendly at first. Then they begin to steal things from the crew. Drake sails on to the Spice Islands.

Spices are very valuable in the 16th century. Drake lands on Ternate, one of the main islands. The Sultan (king) of Ternate makes him very welcome. He offers new supplies for the *Golden Hind*. He gives Drake five tonnes of spices. In return, the Sultan wants English **merchants** to trade with Ternate.

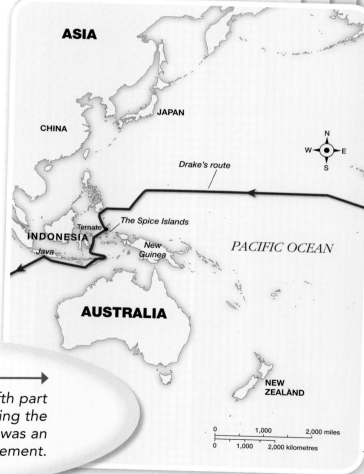

This map shows the fifth part of Drake's voyage. Crossing the Pacific in two months was an amazing achievement.

22

cross-staff   tool for measuring the position of the Sun or stars in the sky
merchants   people who buy and sell things for a living

Finding the way

In the 16th century, it was difficult for sailors to find their way at sea. Drake used a tool called a **cross-staff** to help him (see the picture below). He used a cross-staff to measure the angle between the Sun, or a star, and the horizon. This showed Drake how far north or south he was.

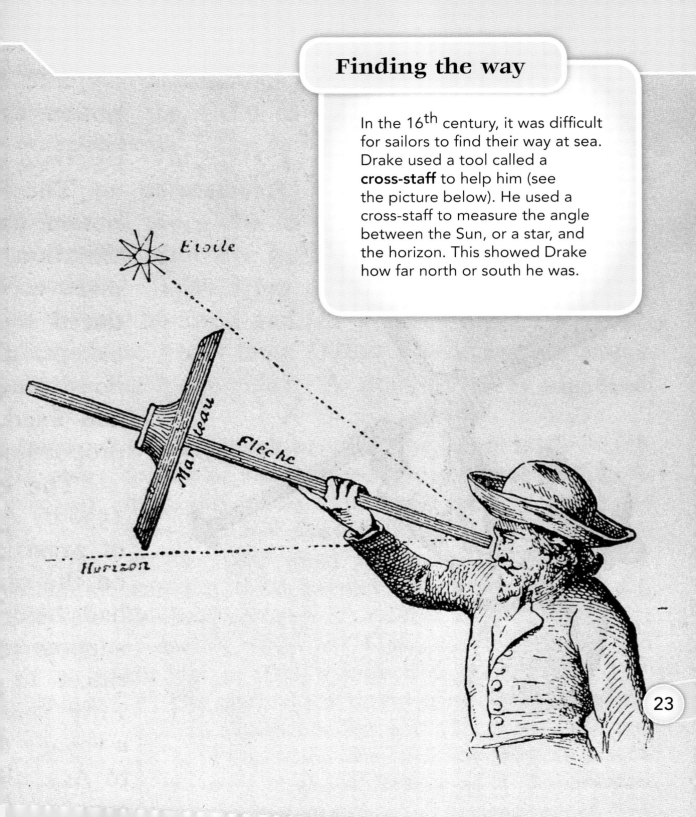

Etoile

Marteau

Flèche

Horizon

Sweat and prayers

The *Golden Hind* sails from Ternate in November 1579. In December it is still among the islands of Indonesia. Then one evening, disaster strikes. The ship runs aground on some rocks.

Luckily, the Golden Hind sailed off the rocks on which it had been stuck, and was able to continue with its long journey. This picture shows a reproduction of the ship.

For nearly a day, Drake and his crew work, worry, sweat, and pray. The ship seems to be stuck fast. But luckily the wind changes. The ship floats off the rocks.

Drake spends several more months in Indonesia. He leaves in April 1580 for another incredible voyage. The *Golden Hind* travels nearly 10,000 miles without stopping. After three months of sailing, Drake arrives in Sierra Leone, Africa, in July.

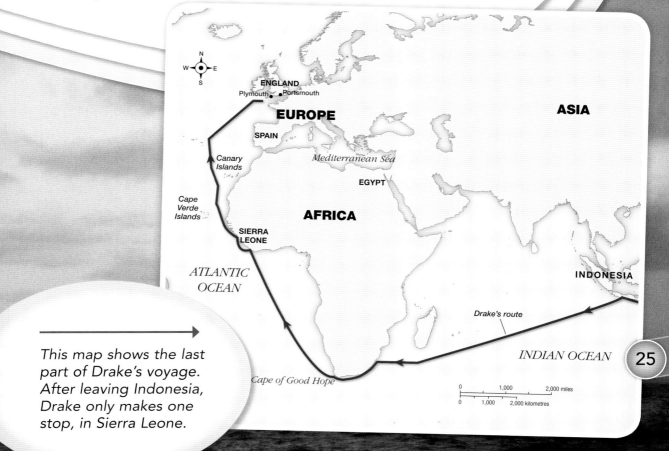

This map shows the last part of Drake's voyage. After leaving Indonesia, Drake only makes one stop, in Sierra Leone.

The queen and the logbook

From Sierra Leone, Drake sails to England without touching land. The *Golden Hind* arrives in Plymouth on 26 September 1580.

The crew are glad to be home. But Drake is worried. England is supposed to be at peace with Spain. The Spanish have heard about Drake's attacks on their ships. They are very angry with Drake for stealing their treasure. They have complained to Queen Elizabeth I. Will the queen be angry with him too?

The queen sends for Drake. She talks with him in private. No one knows what was said. But the queen is certainly not angry. In fact, she makes Drake a **knight**. This is one of the highest honours in the land. Now he is "Sir Francis Drake".

But what happened to Drake's **logbook**? Drake gave it to the queen. She hid it away. It was never seen again! No one was allowed to talk about Drake's adventures or the Spanish treasure. No one wanted to annoy the Spanish!

"Arise Sir Francis!" In this picture, Queen Elizabeth I makes Francis Drake a knight.

knight person who has been honoured by a king or queen

A fabulous treasure

No one knows exactly how much treasure Drake brought back to England. People think it was at least £350,000. This would be billions of pounds in today's money. The queen gave some of it back to Spain. This was because she did not want war with Spain. But Queen Elizabeth I kept most of the treasure. She gave Sir Francis Drake £10,000 for himself, and £10,000 to pay his crew.

Drake's voyage

This map shows all of Drake's voyage. Remember, Tudor ships had no engines. There were no good maps to help sailors find their way. Drake's around-the-world trip was truly amazing!

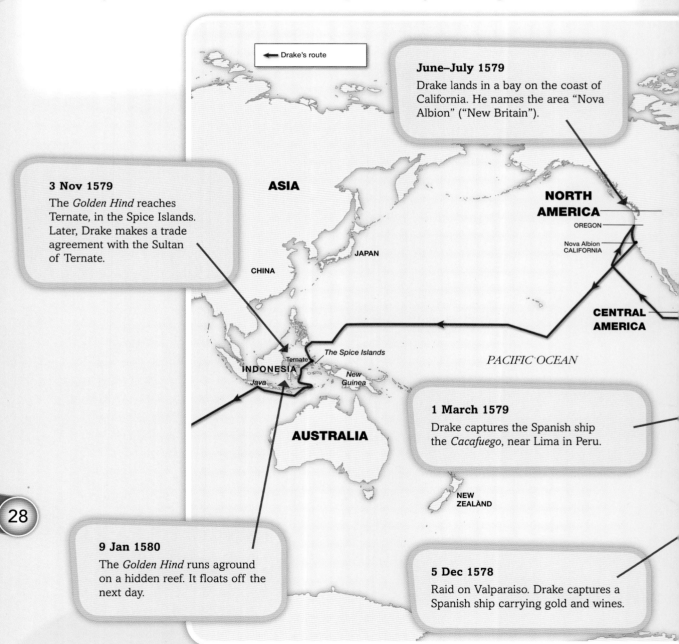

← Drake's route

June–July 1579
Drake lands in a bay on the coast of California. He names the area "Nova Albion" ("New Britain").

3 Nov 1579
The *Golden Hind* reaches Ternate, in the Spice Islands. Later, Drake makes a trade agreement with the Sultan of Ternate.

ASIA

NORTH AMERICA
OREGON
Nova Albion
CALIFORNIA

JAPAN

CHINA

Ternate
The Spice Islands
INDONESIA
Java
New Guinea

CENTRAL AMERICA

PACIFIC OCEAN

1 March 1579
Drake captures the Spanish ship the *Cacafuego*, near Lima in Peru.

AUSTRALIA

NEW ZEALAND

9 Jan 1580
The *Golden Hind* runs aground on a hidden reef. It floats off the next day.

5 Dec 1578
Raid on Valparaiso. Drake captures a Spanish ship carrying gold and wines.

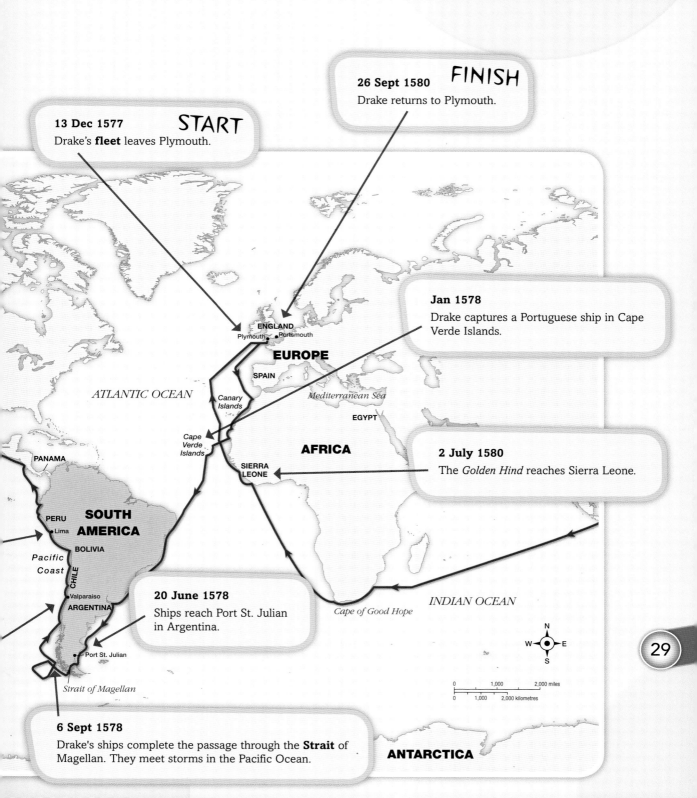

26 Sept 1580 FINISH
Drake returns to Plymouth.

13 Dec 1577 START
Drake's **fleet** leaves Plymouth.

Jan 1578
Drake captures a Portuguese ship in Cape Verde Islands.

2 July 1580
The *Golden Hind* reaches Sierra Leone.

ENGLAND
Plymouth • Portsmouth
EUROPE
SPAIN
Mediterranean Sea
ATLANTIC OCEAN
Canary Islands
EGYPT
Cape Verde Islands
AFRICA
SIERRA LEONE
PANAMA
PERU
• Lima
SOUTH AMERICA
BOLIVIA
Pacific Coast
CHILE
• Valparaiso
ARGENTINA
INDIAN OCEAN
Cape of Good Hope

20 June 1578
Ships reach Port St. Julian in Argentina.

• Port St. Julian
Strait of Magellan

N
W • E
S

0   1,000   2,000 miles
0   1,000   2,000 kilometres

29

6 Sept 1578
Drake's ships complete the passage through the **Strait** of Magellan. They meet storms in the Pacific Ocean.

ANTARCTICA

Glossary

ballast large stones in the bottom of a ship that balance the weight of the masts. Without ballast, a sailing ship would tip over.

behead to kill someone by chopping off their head. This usually happened if someone had broken the law.

colony place that has been conquered and is ruled by a foreign country

cross-staff tool for measuring the position of the Sun or stars in the sky. It helped sailors work out where they were.

explorer person who travels the world to learn about distant lands

figurehead figure at the front part of a ship

fleet group of ships

jury group of people who decide whether someone is guilty or innocent in a trial

knight person who has been honoured by a king or queen. A knight is a noble (upper-class) man. Drake was made a knight (*Sir* Francis Drake) after his voyage around the world.

lead line weight on a thin rope that is thrown over the side of a ship to measure water depth

logbook diary of a sea voyage written by the ship's captain

merchants people who buy and sell things for a living. During Drake's time, merchants explored many new lands looking for goods to trade.

Native Americans the original people of North and South America

pilot on a ship, someone who decides which way a ship should go to reach its destination

ransom money paid to set a prisoner free. Drake ransomed many rich Spaniards that he took prisoner.

reign to rule over a country

settlement town or village

strait narrow strip of water between two pieces of land

treason action that is disloyal to your country. People who commit treason are called traitors.

trial special meeting to decide if someone is guilty or innocent of a crime

Want to know more?

Books to read

Groundbreakers: *Sir Francis Drake*, Neil Champion (Heinemann, 2001)

Horribly Famous: *Sir Francis Drake and His Daring Deeds*, Andrew Donkin (Scholastic, 2006)

People in the Past: *Tudor Exploration*, Haydn Middleton (Heinemann Library, 2003)

Websites

www.activehistory.co.uk / Miscellaneous / free_stuff / google_earth / drake

Fly around the world following Drake's route. See how it looks today, using Google Earth.

www.maryrose.org

Find out about another famous Tudor ship, the *Mary Rose*. Learn about the *Mary Rose*'s history and life on board a sailing ship at the time.

www.nmm.ac.uk / TudorExploration / NMMFLASH / index.htm

Find out more about Tudor exploration with Sir Water Rowdant and his servant Bilge.

Find out more about the Tudors and the way they lived in *Posh Palaces and Horrible Hovels*.

Read about the smelly river Thames in *The Great Stink*.

Index